EMMANUEL JOSEPH

The Fabric of Success, Weaving Together Holistic Growth, Financial Abundance, and Emotional Well-being

Copyright © 2025 by Emmanuel Joseph

All rights reserved. No part of this publication may be reproduced, stored or transmitted in any form or by any means, electronic, mechanical, photocopying, recording, scanning, or otherwise without written permission from the publisher. It is illegal to copy this book, post it to a website, or distribute it by any other means without permission.

First edition

This book was professionally typeset on Reedsy. Find out more at reedsy.com

Contents

1	Chapter 1: The Foundations of Holistic Success	1
2	Chapter 2: Setting Clear and Meaningful Goals	3
3	Chapter 3: The Power of Positive Thinking	5
4	Chapter 4: Financial Abundance and Wealth Management	7
5	Chapter 5: Building and Maintaining Healthy Relationships	9
6	Chapter 6: The Role of Self-Care in Emotional Well-being	11
7	Chapter 7: The Importance of Work-Life Balance	13
8	Chapter 8: The Pursuit of Lifelong Learning	15
9	Chapter 9: Cultivating Resilience and Overcoming Obstacles	17
10	Chapter 10: The Significance of Mindfulness and Meditation	19
11	Chapter 11: The Art of Effective Time Management	21
12	Chapter 12: Building a Strong Personal Brand	23
13	Chapter 13: Navigating Career Transitions and Growth	25
14	Chapter 14: The Intersection of Purpose and Passion	27
15	Chapter 15: The Journey to Holistic Success	29

1

Chapter 1: The Foundations of Holistic Success

Success is a multifaceted concept that extends beyond financial wealth and professional achievements. It encompasses various dimensions, including personal growth, emotional well-being, and meaningful relationships. To truly succeed, one must first understand that these elements are interconnected and form the foundation of holistic success. A balanced approach that nurtures the mind, body, and spirit is essential to achieving a fulfilling life.

The journey toward holistic success begins with self-awareness. Understanding one's values, strengths, and weaknesses is crucial in setting meaningful goals and making informed decisions. By fostering a deep sense of self-awareness, individuals can align their actions with their true purpose and passions. This alignment creates a sense of harmony and authenticity, which is the cornerstone of holistic success.

Another critical aspect of holistic success is the cultivation of emotional intelligence. Emotional intelligence involves the ability to recognize, understand, and manage one's emotions, as well as the emotions of others. This skill is vital in building healthy relationships, navigating challenges, and fostering a positive mindset. By developing emotional intelligence, individuals can create a supportive and nurturing environment that promotes personal and professional growth.

Holistic success also requires a commitment to lifelong learning and personal development. Embracing a growth mindset, where challenges are viewed as opportunities for growth, enables individuals to continuously evolve and adapt. This mindset fosters resilience and perseverance, which are essential qualities for overcoming obstacles and achieving long-term success.

2

Chapter 2: Setting Clear and Meaningful Goals

Goal setting is a fundamental component of achieving success. However, it is not enough to set arbitrary goals; they must be clear, specific, and meaningful. Meaningful goals are those that resonate with an individual's core values and passions. They provide a sense of purpose and direction, guiding one's actions toward a fulfilling and successful life.

To set meaningful goals, one must first identify their core values and priorities. This process involves introspection and self-reflection, allowing individuals to gain clarity on what truly matters to them. By aligning goals with their values, individuals can ensure that their efforts are focused on what brings them the most fulfillment and satisfaction.

Once meaningful goals are identified, it is essential to break them down into smaller, manageable steps. This approach makes the goals more attainable and less overwhelming. By creating a detailed action plan, individuals can track their progress and stay motivated. Each small step taken toward the goal reinforces a sense of accomplishment and drives momentum.

Moreover, setting clear and meaningful goals requires a balance between ambition and realism. While it is important to aim high and challenge oneself, the goals should also be realistic and achievable. Setting unattainable goals can lead to frustration and burnout, whereas achievable goals foster a sense of progress and confidence. Striking this balance ensures that individuals remain motivated and committed to their journey toward success.

3

Chapter 3: The Power of Positive Thinking

Positive thinking is a powerful tool that can significantly impact one's journey toward success. It involves maintaining an optimistic and constructive mindset, even in the face of challenges and setbacks. Positive thinking does not mean ignoring difficulties, but rather approaching them with a solution-oriented attitude. This mindset fosters resilience, creativity, and a sense of empowerment.

One of the key benefits of positive thinking is its ability to reduce stress and improve overall well-being. By focusing on the positive aspects of situations, individuals can mitigate the negative effects of stress and maintain a sense of calm and balance. Positive thinking also enhances mental clarity and decision-making, enabling individuals to navigate challenges more effectively.

Positive thinking also plays a crucial role in building self-confidence and self-esteem. By cultivating a positive self-image and believing in one's abilities, individuals can overcome self-doubt and take bold actions toward their goals. This self-assurance is essential for taking risks, embracing new opportunities, and achieving success.

To harness the power of positive thinking, individuals can practice gratitude and mindfulness. Gratitude involves recognizing and appreciating the positive aspects of life, which fosters a sense of contentment and joy.

Mindfulness, on the other hand, involves being present in the moment and fully engaged in one's experiences. These practices help individuals maintain a positive and balanced perspective, even in challenging times.

4

Chapter 4: Financial Abundance and Wealth Management

Financial abundance is an integral aspect of holistic success. It provides the resources and freedom to pursue one's passions, support loved ones, and contribute to society. However, achieving financial abundance requires effective wealth management and a strategic approach to financial planning.

Wealth management begins with setting clear financial goals and creating a budget. This involves assessing one's income, expenses, and savings to develop a comprehensive financial plan. By setting realistic financial goals and adhering to a budget, individuals can ensure that they are on track to achieve financial stability and growth.

Another critical component of wealth management is investing. Investing allows individuals to grow their wealth over time and create multiple streams of income. It is important to diversify investments across different asset classes, such as stocks, bonds, real estate, and mutual funds, to mitigate risk and maximize returns. Seeking the guidance of a financial advisor can help individuals make informed investment decisions and build a robust portfolio.

Moreover, financial abundance requires disciplined saving and prudent spending. By cultivating healthy financial habits, such as saving a portion of one's income and avoiding unnecessary debt, individuals can build a strong financial foundation. It is also important to continuously educate oneself about personal finance and stay informed about market trends and opportunities.

5

Chapter 5: Building and Maintaining Healthy Relationships

Healthy relationships are a cornerstone of holistic success. They provide emotional support, companionship, and a sense of belonging. Building and maintaining healthy relationships requires effective communication, empathy, and mutual respect. These qualities foster trust, understanding, and deep connections with others.

Effective communication is essential in nurturing healthy relationships. It involves active listening, expressing oneself clearly, and being open to feedback. By practicing active listening, individuals can demonstrate empathy and understanding, which strengthens the bond with others. Clear and honest communication also helps resolve conflicts and misunderstandings, creating a harmonious and supportive environment.

Empathy is another vital quality in building healthy relationships. Empathy involves putting oneself in another person's shoes and understanding their emotions and perspectives. By cultivating empathy, individuals can create deeper connections and foster a sense of compassion and support. Empathy also promotes inclusivity and acceptance, which are essential for building diverse and enriching relationships.

Mutual respect is the foundation of any healthy relationship. It involves valuing each other's opinions, boundaries, and individuality. By showing respect and appreciation, individuals can create a positive and nurturing environment that encourages personal growth and collaboration. Mutual respect also fosters trust and loyalty, which are crucial for maintaining long-lasting relationships.

6

Chapter 6: The Role of Self-Care in Emotional Well-being

Self-care is a fundamental aspect of emotional well-being. It involves taking deliberate actions to nurture one's physical, mental, and emotional health. Self-care practices promote balance, reduce stress, and enhance overall well-being. By prioritizing self-care, individuals can maintain their energy, focus, and resilience, which are essential for achieving holistic success.

Physical self-care involves activities that promote physical health and vitality. This includes regular exercise, a balanced diet, adequate sleep, and routine medical check-ups. By taking care of one's physical health, individuals can boost their energy levels, improve their mood, and enhance their overall quality of life. Physical self-care also plays a crucial role in preventing illness and maintaining long-term health.

Mental self-care involves activities that stimulate and challenge the mind. This includes engaging in hobbies, learning new skills, reading, and practicing mindfulness. Mental self-care promotes cognitive function, creativity, and emotional balance. It also helps individuals manage stress and maintain a positive outlook on life.

Emotional self-care involves activities that nurture one's emotional health and well-being. This includes spending time with loved ones, practicing gratitude, seeking therapy or counseling, and engaging in activities that bring joy and fulfillment. Emotional self-care fosters resilience, self-compassion, and a sense of inner peace. By prioritizing emotional self-care, individuals can enhance their overall well-being and achieve holistic success.

7

Chapter 7: The Importance of Work-Life Balance

Achieving a work-life balance is essential for holistic success. It involves creating harmony between one's professional responsibilities and personal life. A healthy work-life balance promotes well-being, reduces stress, and enhances productivity. By setting boundaries and prioritizing self-care, individuals can achieve a fulfilling and balanced life.

Setting boundaries is a critical aspect of achieving a work-life balance. This involves clearly defining the limits between work and personal life. By setting boundaries, individuals can ensure that they allocate time and energy to both their professional responsibilities and personal pursuits. This balance creates a sense of harmony and prevents burnout.

Another important aspect of work-life balance is time management. Effective time management involves prioritizing tasks, setting realistic deadlines, and avoiding procrastination. By managing time efficiently, individuals can ensure that they complete their work responsibilities without compromising their personal life. Time management also allows individuals to allocate time for self-care, hobbies, and spending time with loved ones.

Moreover, achieving a work-life balance requires self-compassion and flexibility. It is important to recognize that perfection is unattainable and that it is okay to make mistakes. By practicing self-compassion, individuals can reduce stress and maintain a positive mindset. Flexibility also allows individuals to adapt to changing circumstances and find creative solutions to balance their responsibilities.

8

Chapter 8: The Pursuit of Lifelong Learning

Lifelong learning is a key component of holistic success. It involves continuously seeking knowledge, skills, and experiences that promote personal and professional growth. Lifelong learning fosters curiosity, adaptability, and resilience. By embracing a growth mindset, individuals can achieve continuous development and fulfillment.

The pursuit of lifelong learning begins with a curious and open mindset, individuals can continuously seek new experiences and knowledge. This involves stepping out of one's comfort zone and embracing challenges as opportunities for growth. By cultivating a mindset of curiosity and openness, individuals can discover new passions and interests that enrich their lives.

Formal education is just one avenue for lifelong learning. Informal learning, such as reading books, attending workshops, and engaging in hobbies, also plays a significant role in personal development. These activities provide valuable knowledge and skills that can enhance one's personal and professional life. Additionally, seeking mentorship and learning from others' experiences can provide valuable insights and guidance.

Lifelong learning also involves staying informed about trends and developments in one's field of interest. This requires continuous engagement with relevant literature, attending conferences, and participating in professional networks. By staying informed, individuals can adapt to changes and remain competitive in their careers. This proactive approach to learning fosters resilience and adaptability, which are essential for achieving long-term success.

Moreover, lifelong learning promotes a sense of fulfillment and purpose. It provides a sense of accomplishment and satisfaction that comes from mastering new skills and achieving personal growth. By embracing a mindset of lifelong learning, individuals can create a rich and fulfilling life that is marked by continuous growth and development.

9

Chapter 9: Cultivating Resilience and Overcoming Obstacles

Resilience is the ability to bounce back from setbacks and navigate challenges with strength and perseverance. It is a crucial quality for achieving success, as it enables individuals to overcome obstacles and maintain a positive outlook. Cultivating resilience involves developing a mindset that views challenges as opportunities for growth and learning.

One of the key strategies for building resilience is practicing self-compassion. This involves being kind and understanding toward oneself, especially during difficult times. By treating oneself with compassion, individuals can reduce negative self-talk and maintain a positive mindset. Self-compassion also fosters emotional healing and helps individuals cope with stress and adversity.

Another important aspect of resilience is developing a strong support network. Surrounding oneself with supportive and encouraging individuals can provide valuable emotional support and guidance. This network can include friends, family, mentors, and professional counselors. By seeking support and sharing one's experiences, individuals can gain new perspectives and find strength in their connections with others.

Resilience also involves adopting healthy coping mechanisms to manage stress and adversity. This can include practices such as mindfulness, meditation, exercise, and creative expression. These activities promote emotional well-being and provide an outlet for processing difficult emotions. By developing healthy coping mechanisms, individuals can navigate challenges with greater ease and maintain their well-being.

10

Chapter 10: The Significance of Mindfulness and Meditation

Mindfulness and meditation are powerful practices that promote emotional well-being and personal growth. They involve cultivating a state of present-moment awareness and non-judgmental acceptance of one's thoughts and feelings. These practices enhance mental clarity, reduce stress, and foster a sense of inner peace.

Mindfulness involves paying attention to the present moment with a sense of curiosity and openness. It can be practiced in everyday activities, such as eating, walking, and listening. By being fully present in these moments, individuals can enhance their awareness and appreciation of life's experiences. Mindfulness also helps individuals become more attuned to their emotions and reactions, which promotes emotional regulation and resilience.

Meditation is a formal practice that involves focused attention and relaxation. There are various forms of meditation, including mindfulness meditation, loving-kindness meditation, and transcendental meditation. Each form has its unique benefits and can be tailored to individual preferences and needs. Regular meditation practice has been shown to reduce stress, improve concentration, and enhance overall well-being.

Incorporating mindfulness and meditation into daily life can have profound effects on one's mental and emotional health. These practices promote self-awareness, compassion, and a sense of inner calm. By dedicating time to mindfulness and meditation, individuals can create a foundation of emotional well-being that supports their journey toward holistic success.

11

Chapter 11: The Art of Effective Time Management

Effective time management is a crucial skill for achieving success in both personal and professional life. It involves prioritizing tasks, setting goals, and allocating time efficiently to maximize productivity and achieve a balanced lifestyle. By mastering time management, individuals can reduce stress, enhance focus, and achieve their goals more effectively.

One of the key strategies for effective time management is prioritizing tasks based on their importance and urgency. This involves identifying high-priority tasks that align with one's goals and values and focusing on them first. By prioritizing tasks, individuals can ensure that they are dedicating their time and energy to what truly matters.

Another important aspect of time management is setting clear and realistic goals. This involves breaking down larger goals into smaller, manageable tasks and creating a detailed action plan. By setting specific and achievable goals, individuals can track their progress and stay motivated. Clear goals also provide a sense of direction and purpose, which enhances focus and productivity.

Moreover, effective time management requires minimizing distractions and avoiding procrastination. This involves creating a conducive work environment, setting boundaries, and practicing self-discipline. By reducing distractions and staying focused on the task at hand, individuals can achieve higher levels of productivity and efficiency. Additionally, taking regular breaks and practicing self-care is essential for maintaining energy and preventing burnout.

12

Chapter 12: Building a Strong Personal Brand

A strong personal brand is essential for achieving professional success and standing out in a competitive market. It involves showcasing one's unique strengths, values, and expertise to create a positive and memorable impression. Building a personal brand requires authenticity, consistency, and strategic self-presentation.

The foundation of a strong personal brand is self-awareness. This involves understanding one's unique strengths, values, and passions. By identifying what sets them apart, individuals can create a clear and authentic brand identity. Self-awareness also helps individuals align their actions and decisions with their personal brand, which enhances credibility and trust.

Another important aspect of building a personal brand is effective communication. This involves conveying one's message clearly and confidently through various channels, such as social media, networking events, and professional profiles. By consistently communicating their unique value proposition, individuals can build a strong and recognizable brand presence.

Consistency is key in maintaining a strong personal brand. This involves ensuring that all aspects of one's professional presence, from online profiles to personal interactions, reflect their brand identity. Consistency creates a sense of reliability and trust, which are essential for building a positive reputation. Additionally, seeking feedback and continuously refining one's brand can enhance its impact and effectiveness.

13

Chapter 13: Navigating Career Transitions and Growth

Career transitions are an inevitable part of professional life. Whether it involves changing industries, pursuing new opportunities, or seeking advancement, navigating career transitions requires strategic planning and adaptability. By approaching career transitions with a growth mindset, individuals can achieve professional success and fulfillment.

One of the key strategies for navigating career transitions is conducting thorough research and self-assessment. This involves understanding the requirements and opportunities in the desired field and assessing one's skills, strengths, and areas for improvement. By gaining clarity on their career goals and aligning them with their strengths, individuals can make informed decisions and pursue opportunities that align with their aspirations.

Networking is another crucial aspect of navigating career transitions. Building and maintaining professional relationships can provide valuable insights, guidance, and opportunities. Networking involves reaching out to industry professionals, attending events, and leveraging online platforms to connect with others. By seeking mentorship and learning from others' experiences, individuals can gain valuable support and insights during their career transitions.

Moreover, career transitions require a proactive approach to skill development and continuous learning. This involves seeking opportunities for professional development, such as training programs, certifications, and workshops. By continuously enhancing their skills and knowledge, individuals can remain competitive and adaptable in a changing job market. Embracing a growth mindset and viewing challenges as opportunities for growth can also foster resilience and motivation during career transitions.

14

Chapter 14: The Intersection of Purpose and Passion

Finding a sense of purpose and passion is essential for achieving holistic success. Purpose provides a sense of direction and meaning, while passion fuels motivation and enthusiasm. The intersection of purpose and passion creates a fulfilling and rewarding life, where individuals can achieve their goals while making a positive impact.

The journey to finding purpose and passion begins with self-exploration. This involves reflecting on one's values, interests, and experiences to gain clarity on what brings joy and fulfillment. By identifying their core passions and aligning them with their values, individuals can create a sense of purpose that guides their actions and decisions.

Once individuals have identified their purpose and passion, it is important to integrate them into their personal and professional life. This involves pursuing opportunities and activities that align with their passions and contribute to their sense of purpose. By doing so, individuals can create a harmonious and fulfilling life where their actions are in alignment with their true selves.

Moreover, finding purpose and passion requires embracing a mindset of curiosity and openness. This involves being open to new experiences and opportunities, even if they are outside one's comfort zone. By exploring different interests and passions, individuals can discover new paths and possibilities that enrich their lives. Embracing change and adaptability also fosters a sense of resilience and growth, which are essential for achieving holistic success.

15

Chapter 15: The Journey to Holistic Success

The journey to holistic success is a continuous and evolving process that involves integrating various aspects of one's life. It requires a balanced approach that nurtures personal growth, financial abundance, and emotional well-being. By embracing a holistic perspective, individuals can achieve a fulfilling and meaningful life.

The first step in the journey to holistic success is self-awareness. This involves gaining clarity on one's values, strengths, and goals. By understanding themselves on a deeper level, individuals can make informed decisions and take actions that align with their true purpose. Self-awareness also fosters a sense of authenticity and harmony, which are essential for holistic success.

Another important aspect of the journey is setting clear and meaningful goals. This involves identifying what truly matters and creating a plan to achieve it. By setting specific and realistic goals, individuals can track their progress and stay motivated. This approach creates a sense of purpose and direction, guiding individuals toward their desired outcomes. Clear goals also provide a benchmark for measuring success and celebrating achievements along the way.

Another key element in the journey to holistic success is cultivating a positive mindset. This involves maintaining optimism, resilience, and a solution-oriented attitude. By focusing on the positive aspects of situations and viewing challenges as opportunities for growth, individuals can overcome obstacles and achieve their goals. A positive mindset also fosters emotional well-being and enhances overall quality of life.

Holistic success also requires nurturing meaningful relationships and a supportive network. Building strong connections with others provides emotional support, encouragement, and a sense of belonging. These relationships contribute to one's overall well-being and create a positive and enriching environment. By fostering healthy relationships, individuals can enhance their personal and professional growth.

Lastly, the journey to holistic success involves continuous self-improvement and personal development. Embracing lifelong learning, seeking new experiences, and setting new goals ensure that individuals remain dynamic and adaptable. This commitment to growth and development creates a fulfilling and meaningful life, where individuals can achieve their full potential and make a positive impact on the world.

Book Description

"The Fabric of Success: Weaving Together Holistic Growth, Financial Abundance, and Emotional Well-being" is a comprehensive guide to achieving a balanced and fulfilling life. This book explores the interconnected dimensions of holistic growth, financial abundance, and emotional well-being, providing practical strategies and insights to help readers achieve their goals.

Through 15 thoughtfully crafted chapters, readers will learn the importance of self-awareness, goal setting, positive thinking, and effective time management. The book delves into essential topics such as building healthy relationships, cultivating resilience, and navigating career transitions. It also emphasizes the significance of self-care, mindfulness, and continuous learning in achieving holistic success.

Each chapter is designed to provide actionable advice and inspiration, empowering readers to take charge of their lives and create a harmonious and successful future. Whether you are seeking personal growth, financial stability, or emotional well-being, "The Fabric of Success" offers valuable

CHAPTER 15: THE JOURNEY TO HOLISTIC SUCCESS

guidance to help you weave together the fabric of your dreams.

www.ingramcontent.com/pod-product-compliance
Lightning Source LLC
LaVergne TN
LVHW020503080526
838202LV00057B/6122